What's Cooking
pasta

What's Cooking

pasta

A collection of must-have recipes for all occasions

First published in 2010
LOVE FOOD is an imprint of Parragon Books Ltd

Parragon
Queen Street House
4 Queen Street
Bath BA1 1HE, UK

ISBN: 978-1-4454-0318-2

Printed in China

Cover design by Talking Design
Cover image by Clive Streeter
Internal design by Simon Levy
Additional photography by Don Last
Food styling by Christine France
Introduction by Linda Doeser

Notes for the reader

This book uses both metric and imperial measurements. Follow the same units of measurement throughout; do not mix metric and imperial. All spoon measurements are level: teaspoons are assumed to be 5 ml, and tablespoons are assumed to be 15 ml. Unless otherwise stated, milk is assumed to be full fat, eggs and individual vegetables are medium, and pepper is freshly ground black pepper.

The times given are an approximate guide only. Preparation times differ according to the techniques used by different people and the cooking times may also vary from those given. Optional ingredients, variations or serving suggestions have not been included in the calculations.

Recipes using raw or very lightly cooked eggs should be avoided by infants, the elderly, pregnant women, convalescents and anyone suffering from an illness. Pregnant and breastfeeding women are advised to avoid eating peanuts and peanut products. Sufferers from nut allergies should be aware that some of the ready-made ingredients used in the recipes in this book may contain nuts. Always check the packaging before use.

Vegetarians should be aware that some of the ready-made ingredients used in the recipes in this book may contain animal products. Always check the packaging before use.

CONTENTS

INTRODUCTION

Pasta is arguably the most useful ingredient to be found in any kitchen. It goes with just about anything else you can think of – from vegetables and cheese to meat and fish. It's equally delicious served with simple, inexpensive sauces or extravagant and luxurious mixtures, and it can be added to soups or form the basis of filling baked dishes. It may be a main meal, a starter or a delightfully different salad.

Pasta is very versatile so it's easy to find fabulous recipes for all occasions and every season of the year. Virtually everyone loves pasta and it's especially popular with children. High in complex carbohydrates, it provides a steady release of energy but contains hardly any fat. Depending on the type of wheat flour used in its manufacture, it can also be a good source of protein, as well as B vitamins, potassium and iron. Moreover, it's economical, convenient and the dried variety keeps well. Huge numbers of pasta dishes can be prepared and cooked within 30 minutes and many take only half that time.

TYPES OF PASTA

There are hundreds of pasta shapes and new ones are being introduced all the time. There are no hard and fast rules about which shape goes with a particular sauce, although there are some traditional partnerships, such as Spaghetti Bolognese. However, there are some useful guidelines.

Long, thin pasta, such as spaghetti and linguine, is ideal for seafood sauces and light olive oil or fresh tomato dressings, but cannot really hold thick or chunky sauces. These are better served with pasta shapes that trap the sauce in hollows and ridges – penne (quills), fusilli (spirals) or conchiglie (shells), for example. Flat ribbons, such as tagliatelle, fettuccine and pappardelle, are perfect for rich or creamy sauces.

Baked dishes are often made with lasagne (flat sheets of pasta that can be layered with a variety of sauces) or cannelloni (tubes that can be filled and baked in a sauce). Smaller shapes, such as macaroni and rigatoni, are also often used in baking.

Very small pasta shapes, such as stellete (stars) and anellini (rings), are used in soups, and filled pasta, such as ravioli and tortellini, is also often served in broth.

BASIC RECIPES

Béchamel Sauce

Makes 300 ml/10 fl oz

Ingredients
300 ml/10 fl oz milk
1 bay leaf
6 black peppercorns
slice of onion
mace blade
25 g/1 oz butter
25 g/1 oz plain flour
salt and pepper

1 Pour the milk into a saucepan and add the bay leaf, peppercorns, onion and mace. Bring to just below boiling point, then remove the pan from the heat, cover and leave to infuse for 10 minutes. Strain the milk into a jug and discard the flavourings.

2 Melt the butter in another saucepan. Sprinkle in the flour and cook over a low heat, stirring constantly, for 2 minutes. Remove the pan from the heat and gradually stir in the milk.

3 Return the pan to a low heat and bring to the boil, stirring constantly. Cook, stirring constantly, until thickened and smooth. Season to taste with salt and pepper.

Pesto

Serves 4

Ingredients
115 g/4 oz fresh basil leaves
25 g/1 oz pine kernels
1 garlic clove, roughly chopped
55 g/2 oz Parmesan cheese, freshly grated
6–8 tbsp extra virgin olive oil
salt

1 Put the basil, pine kernels and garlic in a mortar. Add a pinch of salt and pound to a paste with a pestle.

2 Transfer the mixture to a bowl and gradually work in the Parmesan cheese with a wooden spoon. Gradually stir in the oil until the sauce is thick and creamy. Cover with clingfilm and store in the refrigerator until required.

MAKING FRESH PASTA

If you want to make filled pasta, such as tortellini, you will need to prepare the dough yourself. The same basic dough can also be used to make lasagne sheets and a variety of shapes, such as tagliatelle, pappardelle and macaroni. You need no special equipment and the process is both easy and satisfying.

Basic pasta dough

Serves 3–4
Preparation time: 15 minutes, plus
30 minutes to rest

Ingredients

200 g/7 oz strong white flour,
  plus extra for dusting
pinch of salt
2 eggs, lightly beaten
1 tbsp olive oil

1 Sift together the flour and salt onto a work surface and make a well in the centre with your fingers. Pour the eggs and oil into the well then, using the fingers of one hand, gradually incorporate the flour into the liquid.

2 Knead the dough on a lightly floured work surface until it is completely smooth. Wrap in clingfilm and leave to rest for 30 minutes before rolling out or feeding through a pasta machine. Resting makes the dough more elastic.

Flavoured pasta

Basic pasta dough may be flavoured and coloured by the addition of other ingredients.

Tomato pasta: Add 2 tablespoons of tomato purée to the well in the flour and use only $1^1/_2$ eggs instead of 2.

Spinach pasta: Blanch 225 g/8 oz spinach in boiling water for 1 minute, then drain and squeeze out as much liquid as possible. Alternatively, use 150 g/5$^1/_2$ oz thawed frozen spinach. This does not need blanching, but as much liquid as possible should be squeezed out. Finely chop the spinach and mix with the flour before making a well and adding the eggs and oil.

Herb pasta: Add 3 tablespoons of finely chopped fresh herbs to the flour before making a well and adding the eggs and oil.

Saffron pasta: Soak a sachet of powdered saffron in 2 tablespoons hot water for 15 minutes. Use $1^1/_2$ eggs and whisk the saffron water into them.

Wholemeal pasta: Use 140 g/5 oz wholemeal flour and 25 g/1 oz strong white flour.

Rolling out pasta dough

When the fresh dough has rested, it may be rolled out by hand or with a pasta machine. Larger quantities of dough should be halved or cut into thirds before rolling out. Keep covered until you are ready to work on them.

To roll out by hand, lightly dust a work surface with plain flour, then roll out the pasta dough with a lightly floured rolling pin, always rolling away from you and turning the dough a quarter turn each time. Keep rolling to make a rectangle 2–3 mm/ $^1/_{16}$–$^1/_8$ inch thick. The dough can then be cut into ribbons, stamped out with a biscuit cutter or cut into squares to make ravioli.

A pasta machine makes rolling out the dough easier and quicker and ensures that it is even. There are a number of models available, the most useful being a hand-cranked machine with attachable cutters. An electric machine is even easier to use but somewhat extravagant. Cut the dough into manageable sized pieces – 1 quantity Basic Pasta Dough should be cut into 4 pieces, for example. Flatten a piece with your hand and wrap the others in clingfilm until required. Fold the flat piece into thirds and feed it through the pasta machine on its widest setting. Repeat the folding and rolling 3 or 4 more times on this setting, then close the rollers by one notch. Continue feeding the dough through the rollers, without folding into thirds, gradually reducing the setting until you reach the narrowest. If you want to make ribbons, cut the dough into 30-cm/12-inch strips and feed through the appropriate cutter.

SOUPS & SALADS

MINESTRONE MILANESE

Heat the oil in a large heavy-based saucepan. Add the pancetta, onions and garlic and cook, stirring occasionally, for 5 minutes. Add the carrots and celery and cook, stirring occasionally, for a further 5 minutes, or until all the vegetables are softened.

Drain the haricot beans and add them to the saucepan with the tomatoes and their can juices and the beef stock. Bring to the boil, reduce the heat, cover and simmer for 1 hour.

Add the potatoes, re-cover and cook for 15 minutes, then add the pasta, green beans, peas, cabbage and parsley. Cover and cook for a further 15 minutes, until all the vegetables are tender. Season to taste with salt and pepper. Ladle into warmed soup bowls and serve immediately with Parmesan cheese shavings.

SERVES 6

2 tbsp olive oil

55 g/2 oz pancetta, diced

2 onions, sliced

2 garlic cloves, finely chopped

3 carrots, chopped

2 celery sticks, chopped

225 g/8 oz haricot beans, soaked for 3–4 hours

400 g/14 oz canned chopped tomatoes

2 litres/3½ pints beef stock

350 g/12 oz potatoes, diced

175 g/6 oz dried macaroni

175 g/6 oz green beans, sliced

115 g/4 oz fresh or frozen peas

225 g/8 oz Savoy cabbage, shredded

3 tbsp chopped fresh flat-leaf parsley

salt and pepper

fresh Parmesan cheese shavings, to serve

ITALIAN
CHICKEN SOUP

Place the chicken in a large saucepan and pour in the chicken stock and cream. Bring to the boil, then reduce the heat and simmer for 20 minutes.

Meanwhile, bring a large heavy-based saucepan of lightly salted water to the boil. Add the pasta, return to the boil and cook for 8–10 minutes, or until just tender but still firm to the bite. Drain the pasta well and keep warm.

Season the soup with salt and pepper to taste. Mix the cornflour and milk together until a smooth paste forms, then stir it into the soup. Add the sweetcorn and pasta and heat through. Ladle the soup into warmed soup bowls and serve.

SERVES 4

450 g/1 lb skinless, boneless chicken breasts, cut into thin strips

1.2 litres/2 pints chicken stock

150 ml/5 fl oz double cream

115 g/4 oz dried vermicelli

1 tbsp cornflour

3 tbsp milk

175 g/6 oz canned sweetcorn kernels, drained

salt and pepper

CHICKEN & PASTA BROTH

Put the chicken into a large flameproof casserole dish with the water, celery, carrot, onion, leek, garlic, peppercorns, allspice, herbs and ½ teaspoon of salt. Bring just to the boil over a medium heat and skim off the scum that rises to the surface. Reduce the heat, partially cover and simmer for 2 hours.

Remove the chicken from the stock and leave to cool. Continue simmering the stock, uncovered, for about 30 minutes. When the chicken is cool enough to handle, remove the meat from the bones and, if necessary, cut into bite-sized pieces.

Strain the stock and remove as much fat as possible. Discard the vegetables and flavourings. (There should be about 1.7 litres/3 pints chicken stock.)

Bring the stock to the boil in a clean pan over a medium heat. Add the pasta and reduce the heat so the stock simmers very gently. Cook for 8–10 minutes, or until the pasta is tender but still firm to the bite.

Stir in the chicken. Taste and adjust the seasoning. Ladle into bowls, sprinkle with parsley and serve.

SERVES 4–6

1.25 kg/2 lb 12 oz chicken pieces, such as wings or legs

2.5 litres/4½ pints water

1 celery stick, sliced

1 large carrot, sliced

1 onion, sliced

1 leek, sliced

2 garlic cloves, finely chopped

8 peppercorns

4 allspice berries

3–4 fresh parsley stems

2–3 fresh thyme sprigs

1 bay leaf

85 g/3 oz dried farfalline

salt and pepper

chopped fresh parsley, to garnish

FISH SOUP WITH MACARONI

Heat the oil in a large heavy-based saucepan. Add the onions and garlic and cook over a low heat, stirring occasionally, for 5 minutes, or until the onions have softened.

Add the stock with the tomatoes and their can juices, herbs, saffron and pasta and season to taste with salt and pepper. Bring to the boil, then cover and simmer for 15 minutes.

Discard any mussels with broken shells or any that refuse to close when tapped. Add the mussels, monkfish and prawns to the saucepan. Re-cover the saucepan and simmer for a further 5–10 minutes, until the mussels have opened, the prawns have changed colour and the fish is opaque and flakes easily. Discard any mussels that remain closed. Ladle the soup into warmed bowls and serve.

SERVES 6

2 tbsp olive oil

2 onions, sliced

1 garlic clove, finely chopped

1 litre/1¾ pints fish stock or water

400 g/14 oz canned chopped tomatoes

¼ tsp herbes de Provence

¼ tsp saffron threads

115 g/4 oz dried macaroni

18 live mussels, scrubbed and debearded

450 g/1 lb monkfish fillet, cut into chunks

225 g/8 oz raw prawns, peeled and deveined, tails left on

salt and pepper

PASTA & CHICKEN MEDLEY

To make the dressing, whisk the vinegar and oil together well, then season to taste with salt and pepper.

Bring a large saucepan of lightly salted water to the boil. Add the pasta, bring back to the boil and cook for 8–10 minutes, until tender but still firm to the bite. Drain thoroughly, rinse and drain again. Transfer to a bowl and mix in 1 tablespoon of the dressing while hot, then set aside until cold.

Combine the mayonnaise, pesto and soured cream in a bowl, and season to taste with salt and pepper.

Add the chicken, celery, grapes, carrot and the mayonnaise mixture to the pasta, and toss thoroughly. Check the seasoning, adding more salt and pepper if necessary.

Arrange the pasta mixture in a large serving bowl, garnish with the celery leaves and serve.

SERVES 2

125–150 g/4½–5½ oz dried fusilli

2 tbsp mayonnaise

2 tsp Pesto (see page 7)

1 tbsp soured cream or natural fromage frais

175 g/6 oz cooked skinless, boneless chicken, cut into strips

1–2 celery sticks, sliced diagonally

125 g/4½ oz black grapes, halved and deseeded

1 large carrot, cut into strips

salt and pepper

celery leaves, to garnish

dressing

1 tbsp white wine vinegar

3 tbsp extra virgin olive oil

salt and pepper

RARE BEEF PASTA SALAD

Season the steak to taste with salt and pepper, then grill or pan-fry for 4 minutes on each side. Leave to rest for 5 minutes, then, using a sharp knife, slice the steak thinly across the grain and reserve until required.

Meanwhile, bring a large pan of lightly salted water to the boil over a medium heat. Add the pasta and cook for 8–10 minutes, until tender but still firm to the bite. Drain thoroughly, refresh in cold water and drain again. Toss the pasta in the oil.

Mix the lime juice, fish sauce and honey together in a small pan and cook over a medium heat for about 2 minutes.

Add the spring onions, cucumber, tomato wedges and mint to the pan, then add the steak and mix well. Season with salt to taste.

Transfer the pasta to a large warmed serving dish and top with the steak mixture. Serve just warm or leave to cool completely.

SERVES 4

450 g/1 lb rump or sirloin
    steak in 1 piece

450 g/1 lb dried fusilli

4 tbsp olive oil

2 tbsp lime juice

2 tbsp Thai fish sauce

2 tsp clear honey

4 spring onions, sliced

1 cucumber, peeled and cut into
    2.5-cm/1-inch chunks

3 tomatoes, cut into wedges

3 tsp finely chopped fresh mint

salt and pepper

SPICY SAUSAGE SALAD

Bring a pan of lightly salted water to the boil over a medium heat. Add the pasta and cook for 8–10 minutes, or until tender but still firm to the bite. Drain thoroughly and reserve.

Heat the oil in a pan over a medium heat. Add the onion and cook until translucent. Stir in the garlic, yellow pepper and sausage and cook for about 3–4 minutes, stirring once or twice.

Add the wine, vinegar and reserved pasta to the pan, stir and bring the mixture just to the boil over a medium heat.

Arrange the salad leaves on large serving plates, spoon over the warm sausage and pasta mixture and serve immediately.

SERVES 4

125 g/4½ oz dried conchiglie

2 tbsp olive oil

1 medium onion, chopped

2 garlic cloves, very finely chopped

1 small yellow pepper, deseeded and cut into matchsticks

175 g/6 oz spicy pork sausage, such as chorizo, Italian pepperoni or salami, skinned and sliced

2 tbsp red wine

1 tbsp red wine vinegar

125 g/4½ oz mixed salad leaves

salt

SPAGHETTI WITH MEATBALLS

Place the potato in a small pan, add cold water to cover and a pinch of salt and bring to the boil. Cook for 10–15 minutes, until tender, then drain. Either mash thoroughly with a potato masher or fork, or pass through a potato ricer.

Combine the potato, beef, onion, egg and parsley in a bowl and season to taste with salt and pepper. Spread out the flour on a plate. With dampened hands, shape the meat mixture into walnut-sized balls and roll in the flour. Shake off any excess.

Heat the oil in a heavy-based frying pan, add the meatballs and cook over a medium heat, stirring and turning frequently, for 8–10 minutes, until golden all over.

Add the passata and tomato purée and cook for a further 10 minutes, until the sauce is reduced and thickened.

Meanwhile, bring a large saucepan of lightly salted water to the boil. Add the pasta, bring back to the boil and cook for 8–10 minutes, or until tender but still firm to the bite.

Drain well and add to the meatball sauce, tossing well to coat. Transfer to a warmed serving dish, garnish with the basil and serve immediately with freshly grated Parmesan cheese.

SERVES 6

1 potato, diced

400 g/14 oz fresh beef mince

1 onion, finely chopped

1 egg

4 tbsp chopped fresh flat-leaf parsley

plain flour, for dusting

5 tbsp olive oil

400 ml/14 fl oz passata

2 tbsp tomato purée

400 g/14 oz dried spaghetti

salt and pepper

shredded fresh basil, to garnish

freshly grated Parmesan cheese, to serve

SPAGHETTI ALLA CARBONARA

Bring a large heavy-based saucepan of lightly salted water to the boil. Add the pasta, return to the boil and cook for 8–10 minutes, or until tender but still firm to the bite.

Meanwhile, heat the oil in a heavy-based frying pan. Add the pancetta and cook over a medium heat, stirring frequently, for 8–10 minutes.

Beat the eggs with the cream in a small bowl and season to taste with salt and pepper. Drain the pasta and return it to the saucepan. Tip in the contents of the frying pan, then add the egg mixture and half the Parmesan cheese. Stir well, then transfer to a warmed serving dish. Serve immediately, sprinkled with the remaining cheese.

SERVES 4

450 g/1 lb dried spaghetti

1 tbsp olive oil

225 g/8 oz rindless pancetta or streaky bacon, chopped

4 eggs

5 tbsp single cream

2 tbsp freshly grated Parmesan cheese

salt and pepper

LINGUINE WITH BACON & OLIVES

Heat the oil in a large frying pan. Add the onions, garlic and bacon and cook over a low heat, stirring occasionally, until the onions are softened. Stir in the mushrooms, anchovies and olives, then season to taste with salt, if necessary, and pepper. Simmer for 5 minutes.

Meanwhile, bring a large heavy-based saucepan of lightly salted water to the boil. Add the pasta, return to the boil and cook for 8–10 minutes, or until tender but still firm to the bite.

Drain the pasta and transfer to a warmed serving dish. Spoon the sauce on top, toss lightly and sprinkle with the Parmesan cheese. Serve immediately.

SERVES 4

3 tbsp olive oil

2 onions, thinly sliced

2 garlic cloves, finely chopped

175 g/6 oz rindless lean bacon, diced

225 g/8 oz mushrooms, sliced

5 canned anchovy fillets, drained

6 black olives, stoned and halved

450 g/1 lb dried linguine

25 g/1 oz freshly grated Parmesan cheese

salt and pepper

PENNE WITH HAM, TOMATO & CHILLI SAUCE

Put the oil and 1 tablespoon of the butter in a large saucepan over a medium–low heat. Add the onion and cook for 10 minutes, or until soft and golden. Add the ham and cook for 5 minutes, or until lightly browned. Stir in the garlic, chilli and tomatoes. Season to taste with salt and pepper. Bring to the boil, then simmer over a medium–low heat for 30–40 minutes, until thickened.

Meanwhile, bring a large heavy-based saucepan of lightly salted water to the boil. Add the pasta, return to the boil and cook for 8–10 minutes, or until tender but still firm to the bite. Drain and transfer to a warmed serving dish.

Pour the sauce over the pasta. Add the parsley, Parmesan cheese and the remaining butter. Toss well to mix and serve immediately.

SERVES 4

1 tbsp olive oil

2 tbsp butter

1 onion, finely chopped

150 g/5½ oz ham, diced

2 garlic cloves, very finely chopped

1 fresh red chilli, deseeded and finely chopped

800 g/1 lb 12 oz canned chopped tomatoes

450 g/1 lb dried penne

2 tbsp chopped fresh flat-leaf parsley

6 tbsp freshly grated Parmesan cheese

salt and pepper

FARFALLE WITH GORGONZOLA & HAM

Pour the crème fraîche into a saucepan, add the mushrooms and season to taste with salt and pepper. Bring to just below the boil, then lower the heat and simmer very gently, stirring occasionally, for 8–10 minutes, until thickened.

Meanwhile, bring a large pan of lightly salted water to the boil. Add the pasta, bring back to the boil and cook for 8–10 minutes, until tender but still firm to the bite.

Remove the pan containing the mushroom mixture from the heat and stir in the Gorgonzola cheese until it has melted. Return the pan to a very low heat and stir in the chopped parsley and ham.

Drain the pasta and add it to the sauce. Toss lightly, then divide between individual warmed plates, garnish with parsley sprigs and serve.

SERVES 4

225 ml/8 fl oz crème fraîche

225 g/8 oz chestnut mushrooms, quartered

400 g/14 oz dried farfalle

85 g/3 oz Gorgonzola cheese, crumbled

1 tbsp chopped fresh flat-leaf parsley, plus extra sprigs to garnish

175 g/6 oz cooked ham, diced

salt and pepper

PEPPERONI PASTA

Heat 2 tablespoons of the oil in a large heavy-based frying pan. Add the onion and cook over a low heat, stirring occasionally, for 5 minutes, or until softened. Add the red and orange peppers, tomatoes and their can juices, sun-dried tomato paste and paprika and bring to the boil.

Add the pepperoni and parsley and season to taste with salt and pepper. Stir well, bring to the boil, then reduce the heat and simmer for 10–15 minutes.

Meanwhile, bring a large heavy-based saucepan of lightly salted water to the boil. Add the pasta, return to the boil and cook for 8–10 minutes, or until tender but still firm to the bite. Drain well and transfer to a warmed serving dish. Add the remaining olive oil and toss. Add the sauce and toss again. Sprinkle with parsley and serve immediately.

SERVES 4

3 tbsp olive oil

1 onion, chopped

1 red pepper, deseeded and diced

1 orange pepper, deseeded and diced

800 g/1 lb 12 oz canned chopped tomatoes

1 tbsp sun-dried tomato paste

1 tsp paprika

225 g/8 oz pepperoni sausage, sliced

2 tbsp chopped fresh flat-leaf parsley, plus extra to garnish

450 g/1 lb dried penne

salt and pepper

MACARONI WITH SAUSAGE, PEPPERONCINI & OLIVES

Heat the oil in a large frying pan over a medium heat. Add the onion and cook for 5 minutes, until softened. Add the garlic and cook for a few seconds, until just beginning to colour. Add the sausage and cook until evenly browned.

Stir in the pepperoncini, tomatoes, oregano and stock. Season to taste with salt and pepper. Bring to the boil, then simmer over a medium heat for 10 minutes, stirring occasionally.

Meanwhile, bring a large saucepan of lightly salted water to the boil. Add the pasta, bring back to the boil and cook for 8–10 minutes, or until tender but still firm to the bite. Drain and transfer to a warmed serving dish.

Add the olives and half the cheese to the sauce, then stir until the cheese has melted.

Pour the sauce over the pasta. Toss well to mix. Sprinkle with the remaining cheese and serve immediately.

SERVES 6

1 tbsp olive oil

1 large onion, finely chopped

2 garlic cloves, very finely chopped

450 g/1 lb pork sausage, peeled and roughly chopped

3 canned pepperoncini, or other hot red peppers, drained and sliced

400 g/14 oz canned chopped tomatoes

2 tsp dried oregano

125 ml/4 fl oz chicken stock or red wine

450 g/1 lb dried macaroni

12–15 stoned black olives, quartered

75 g/2¾ oz freshly grated cheese, such as Cheddar or Gruyère

salt and pepper

PASTA & PORK IN CREAM SAUCE

To make the red wine sauce, heat the oil in a small heavy-based saucepan, add the onion and cook until translucent. Stir in the tomato purée, red wine and oregano. Heat gently to reduce and set aside.

Pound the slices of pork between 2 sheets of clingfilm until wafer thin, then cut into strips. Heat the oil in a frying pan, add the pork and cook for 5 minutes. Add the mushrooms and cook for a further 2 minutes. Strain and pour over the red wine sauce. Reduce the heat and simmer for 20 minutes.

Meanwhile, bring a large heavy-based saucepan of lightly salted water to the boil. Add the lemon juice, saffron and pasta, return to the boil and cook for 8–10 minutes, or until tender but still firm to the bite. Drain the pasta thoroughly, return to the saucepan and keep warm.

Stir the cream into the saucepan with the pork and heat for a few minutes.

Boil the quail eggs for 3 minutes, cool them in cold water and remove the shells. Transfer the pasta to a large warmed serving plate, top with the pork and the sauce and garnish with the eggs. Serve immediately.

SERVES 4

450 g/1 lb pork fillet, thinly sliced

4 tbsp olive oil

225 g/8 oz button mushrooms, sliced

1 tbsp lemon juice

pinch of saffron threads

350 g/12 oz dried orecchiette

4 tbsp double cream

12 quail eggs

salt

red wine sauce

1 tbsp olive oil

1 onion, chopped

1 tbsp tomato purée

200 ml/7 fl oz red wine

1 tsp finely chopped fresh oregano

PENNE WITH TURKEY MEATBALLS

Put the turkey, garlic and parsley in a bowl and mix well. Stir in the egg and season to taste with salt and pepper. Dust your hands lightly with flour and shape the mixture into walnut-sized balls between your palms. Lightly dust each meatball with flour.

Heat the oil in a saucepan. Add the onion, celery and carrot and cook over a low heat, stirring occasionally, for 5 minutes, until softened. Increase the heat to medium, add the meatballs and cook, turning frequently, for 8–10 minutes, until golden brown all over.

Pour in the passata, add the rosemary and bay leaf, season to taste with salt and pepper and bring to the boil. Lower the heat, cover and simmer gently, stirring occasionally, for 40–45 minutes. Remove and discard the herbs.

Shortly before the meatballs are ready, bring a large pan of lightly salted water to the boil. Add the pasta, bring back to the boil and cook for 8–10 minutes, until tender but still firm to the bite. Drain and add to the pan with the meatballs. Stir gently and heat through briefly, then spoon into individual warmed dishes. Sprinkle generously with Parmesan cheese and serve immediately.

SERVES 4

350 g/12 oz fresh turkey mince

1 small garlic clove, finely chopped

2 tbsp finely chopped fresh
    parsley

1 egg, lightly beaten

plain flour, for dusting

3 tbsp olive oil

1 onion, finely chopped

1 celery stick, finely chopped

1 carrot, finely chopped

400 ml/14 fl oz passata

1 fresh rosemary sprig

1 bay leaf

350 g/12 oz dried penne

salt and pepper

freshly grated Parmesan cheese,
    to serve

FETTUCCINE WITH DUCK SAUCE

Heat half the oil in a frying pan. Add the duck and cook over a medium heat, turning frequently, for 8–10 minutes, until golden brown. Using a slotted spoon, transfer to a large saucepan.

Wipe out the frying pan with kitchen paper, then add the remaining oil. Add the shallot, leek, garlic, celery, carrot and pancetta and cook over a low heat, stirring, for 10 minutes. Using a slotted spoon, transfer the mixture to the pan with the duck and stir in the parsley. Add the bay leaf and season to taste with salt and pepper. Pour in the wine and cook over a high heat, stirring occasionally, until reduced by half. Add the tomatoes, tomato purée and sugar and cook for a further 5 minutes. Pour in just enough water to cover and bring to the boil. Lower the heat, cover and simmer gently for 1 hour, until the duck is cooked through and tender.

Remove the saucepan from the heat and transfer the duck to a chopping board. Skim off the fat from the surface of the sauce and discard the bay leaf. Remove and discard the skin from the duck and cut the meat off the bones, then dice. Return the duck meat to the pan and keep warm.

Bring a large pan of salted water to the boil. Add the pasta, return to the boil and cook for 8–10 minutes, until tender but still firm to the bite. Drain and place in a serving dish. Spoon the sauce over the pasta and serve with Parmesan.

SERVES 4

4 tbsp olive oil

4 duck legs

1 shallot, finely chopped

1 leek, white part only, finely chopped

1 garlic clove, finely chopped

1 celery stick, finely chopped

1 carrot, finely chopped

4 pancetta or bacon slices, diced

1 tbsp finely chopped fresh flat-leaf parsley

1 bay leaf

5 tbsp dry white wine

400 g/14 oz canned chopped tomatoes

2 tbsp tomato purée

pinch of sugar

450 g/1 lb dried fettuccine

salt and pepper

freshly grated Parmesan cheese, to serve

PENNE WITH SICILIAN SAUCE

Soak the sultanas in a bowl of warm water for about 20 minutes. Drain the sultanas thoroughly.

Preheat the grill, then cook the tomatoes under the hot grill for 10 minutes. Leave to cool slightly, then once cool enough to handle, peel off the skin and dice the flesh. Place the pine kernels on a baking tray and lightly toast under the grill for 2–3 minutes, or until golden brown.

Place the tomatoes, pine kernels and sultanas in a small saucepan and heat gently. Add the anchovies and tomato purée, and cook the sauce over a low heat for a further 2–3 minutes, or until hot.

Meanwhile, bring a large heavy-based saucepan of lightly salted water to the boil. Add the pasta, return to the boil and cook for 8–10 minutes, or until tender but still firm to the bite. Drain thoroughly, then transfer the pasta to a serving plate and serve with the Sicilian sauce.

SERVES 4

50 g/1¾ oz sultanas

450 g/1 lb tomatoes, halved

25 g/1 oz pine kernels

50 g/1¾ oz canned anchovies, drained and halved lengthways

2 tbsp tomato purée

350 g/12 oz dried penne

salt

SPINACH & ANCHOVY PASTA

Trim off any tough spinach stalks. Rinse the spinach leaves under cold running water and place them in a large saucepan with only the water that is clinging to them after washing. Cover and cook over a high heat, shaking the saucepan from time to time, until the spinach has wilted, but retains its colour. Drain well, reserve and keep warm.

Bring a large heavy-based saucepan of lightly salted water to the boil. Add the pasta, return to the boil and cook for 8–10 minutes, or until tender but still firm to the bite.

Heat 4 tablespoons of the oil in a separate saucepan. Add the pine kernels and cook until golden. Remove the pine kernels from the saucepan and reserve until required.

Add the garlic to the saucepan and cook until golden. Add the anchovies and stir in the spinach. Cook, stirring, for 2–3 minutes, until heated through. Return the pine kernels to the saucepan.

Drain the pasta, toss in the remaining oil and transfer to a warmed serving dish. Spoon the anchovy and spinach sauce over the pasta, toss lightly and serve immediately.

SERVES 4

900 g/2 lb fresh, young spinach leaves

400 g/14 oz dried fettuccine

5 tbsp olive oil

3 tbsp pine kernels

3 garlic cloves, crushed

8 canned anchovy fillets, drained and chopped

salt

SPRINGTIME PASTA

Fill a bowl with cold water and add the lemon juice. Prepare the artichokes one at a time. Cut off the stems and trim away any tough outer leaves. Cut across the tops of the leaves. Slice in half lengthways and remove the central fibrous chokes, then cut lengthways into 5 mm/¼ inch thick slices. Immediately place the slices in the bowl of acidulated water to prevent discoloration.

Heat 5 tablespoons of the oil in a heavy-based frying pan. Drain the artichoke slices and pat dry with kitchen paper. Add them to the frying pan with the shallots, garlic, parsley and mint and cook over a low heat, stirring frequently, for 10–12 minutes, until tender.

Meanwhile, bring a large saucepan of lightly salted water to the boil. Add the pasta, bring back to the boil and cook for 8–10 minutes, until tender but still firm to the bite.

Peel the prawns, cut a slit along the back of each and remove and discard the dark vein. Melt the butter in a small frying pan and add the prawns. Cook, stirring occasionally, for 2–3 minutes, until they have changed colour. Season to taste with salt and pepper.

Drain the pasta and tip it into a bowl. Add the remaining oil and toss well. Add the artichoke mixture and the prawns and toss again. Serve immediately.

SERVES 4

2 tbsp lemon juice

4 baby globe artichokes

7 tbsp olive oil

2 shallots, finely chopped

2 garlic cloves, finely chopped

2 tbsp chopped fresh flat-leaf parsley

2 tbsp chopped fresh mint

350 g/12 oz dried rigatoni

12 large raw prawns

25 g/1 oz unsalted butter

salt and pepper

TAGLIATELLE IN A CREAMY PRAWN SAUCE

Heat the oil and butter in a saucepan over a medium–low heat. Add the garlic and red pepper. Cook for a few seconds until the garlic is just beginning to colour. Stir in the tomato purée and wine. Cook for 10 minutes, stirring.

Bring a large saucepan of lightly salted water to the boil. Add the pasta, bring back to the boil and cook for 8–10 minutes, or until tender but still firm to the bite. Drain and return to the pan.

Add the prawns to the sauce and increase the heat to medium–high. Cook for 2 minutes, stirring, until the prawns turn pink. Reduce the heat and stir in the cream. Cook for 1 minute, stirring constantly, until thickened. Season to taste with salt and pepper.

Transfer the pasta to a warmed serving dish. Pour the sauce over the pasta. Sprinkle with the parsley. Toss well to mix and serve immediately.

SERVES 4

3 tbsp olive oil

3 tbsp butter

4 garlic cloves, very finely chopped

2 tbsp finely diced red pepper

2 tbsp tomato purée

125 ml/4 fl oz dry white wine

450 g/1 lb dried tagliatelle

350 g/12 oz raw peeled prawns

125 ml/4 fl oz double cream

salt and pepper

3 tbsp chopped fresh flat-leaf parsley, to garnish

LINGUINE WITH PRAWNS & SCALLOPS

Peel and devein the prawns, reserving the shells. Melt the butter in a heavy-based frying pan. Add the shallots and cook over a low heat, stirring occasionally, for 5 minutes, or until softened. Add the prawn shells and cook, stirring constantly, for 1 minute. Pour in the vermouth and cook, stirring, for 1 minute. Add the water, bring to the boil, then reduce the heat and simmer for 10 minutes, or until the liquid has reduced by half. Remove the frying pan from the heat.

Bring a large heavy-based saucepan of lightly salted water to the boil. Add the pasta, return to the boil and cook for 8–10 minutes, or until tender but still firm to the bite.

Meanwhile, heat the oil in a separate heavy-based frying pan. Add the scallops and prawns and cook, stirring frequently, for 2 minutes, or until the scallops are opaque and the prawns have changed colour. Strain the prawn-shell stock into the frying pan. Drain the pasta and add to the frying pan with the chives and season to taste with salt and pepper. Toss well over a low heat for 1 minute, then serve.

SERVES 6

450 g/1 lb raw prawns

25 g/1 oz butter

2 shallots, finely chopped

225 ml/8 fl oz dry white vermouth

350 ml/12 fl oz water

450 g/1 lb dried linguine

2 tbsp olive oil

450 g/1 lb prepared scallops, thawed if frozen

2 tbsp snipped fresh chives

salt and pepper

LINGUINE WITH MIXED SEAFOOD

Heat the oil in a saucepan. Add the shallots, garlic and chilli and cook over a low heat, stirring occasionally, for 5 minutes. Increase the heat to medium, stir in the tomatoes, parsley and sugar and season to taste with salt and pepper. Bring to the boil, then cover and simmer, stirring occasionally, for 15–20 minutes.

Discard any mussels or clams with broken shells or any that refuse to close when tapped. Pour the wine into a large saucepan and add the lemon slices, mussels and clams. Cover and cook over a high heat, shaking the pan occasionally, for 5 minutes, until all the shellfish have opened. Using a slotted spoon, transfer the shellfish to a bowl and reserve the cooking liquid.

Discard any mussels and clams that remain closed. Reserve a few for the garnish and remove the remainder from their shells. Strain the cooking liquid through a muslin-lined sieve.

Bring a saucepan of lightly salted water to the boil. Add the pasta and cook for 8–10 minutes, until tender but still firm to the bite.

Meanwhile, stir the strained cooking liquid into the shallot and tomato mixture and bring to the boil, stirring constantly. Add the shelled mussels and clams and the prawns. Taste and adjust the seasoning, if necessary, and heat through gently.

Strain the pasta and return it to the pan. Add the shellfish mixture and toss well. Serve, garnished with the reserved shellfish and parsley sprigs.

SERVES 4–6

2 tbsp olive oil

2 shallots, finely chopped

2 garlic cloves, finely chopped

1 small red chilli, deseeded and finely chopped

200 g/7 oz canned chopped tomatoes

½ bunch fresh flat-leaf parsley, chopped, plus extra sprigs to garnish

pinch of sugar

450 g/1 lb live mussels, scrubbed and debearded

450 g/1 lb live clams, scrubbed

6 tbsp dry white wine

1 lemon, sliced

450 g/1 lb dried linguine

175 g/6 oz large cooked prawns, shelled and deveined

salt and pepper

SPAGHETTI
WITH CRAB

Using a sharp knife, scoop the meat from the crab shell into a bowl. Mix the white and brown meat together lightly and reserve.

Bring a large pan of lightly salted water to the boil over a medium heat. Add the pasta and cook for 8–10 minutes, or until tender but still firm to the bite. Drain thoroughly and return to the pan.

Meanwhile, heat 2 tablespoons of the oil in a frying pan over a low heat. Add the chilli and garlic and cook for 30 seconds, then add the crabmeat, parsley, lemon juice and lemon rind. Cook for 1 minute, until the crab is just heated through.

Add the crab mixture to the pasta with the remaining oil and season to taste with salt and pepper. Toss together thoroughly, transfer to a large warmed serving dish and garnish with lemon wedges. Serve immediately.

SERVES 4

1 dressed crab, about 450 g/
 1 lb including the shell

350 g/12 oz dried spaghetti

6 tbsp extra virgin olive oil

1 fresh red chilli, deseeded and
 finely chopped

2 garlic cloves, finely chopped

3 tbsp chopped fresh parsley

2 tbsp lemon juice

1 tsp finely grated lemon rind

salt and pepper

lemon wedges, to garnish

PENNE WITH SQUID & TOMATOES

Bring a large heavy-based saucepan of lightly salted water to the boil. Add the pasta, return to the boil and cook for 3 minutes, then drain and reserve until required. With a sharp knife, cut the squid into strips.

Heat the oil in a large saucepan. Add the onions and cook over a low heat, stirring occasionally, for 5 minutes, or until softened. Add the squid and stock, bring to the boil and simmer for 3 minutes. Stir in the wine, tomatoes and their can juices, tomato purée, marjoram and bay leaf. Season to taste with salt and pepper. Bring to the boil and cook for 5 minutes, or until slightly reduced.

Add the pasta, return to the boil and simmer for 5–7 minutes, or until tender but still firm to the bite. Remove and discard the bay leaf. Transfer to a warmed serving dish, garnish with the parsley and serve immediately.

SERVES 4

225 g/8 oz dried penne

350 g/12 oz prepared squid

6 tbsp olive oil

2 onions, sliced

225 ml/8 fl oz fish or chicken stock

150 ml/5 fl oz full-bodied red wine

400 g/14 oz canned chopped tomatoes

2 tbsp tomato purée

1 tbsp chopped fresh marjoram

1 bay leaf

salt and pepper

2 tbsp chopped fresh parsley, to garnish

VEGETARIAN

TAGLIATELLE WITH GARLIC CRUMBS

Mix the breadcrumbs, parsley, chives and marjoram together in a small bowl.

Heat the oil in a large heavy-based frying pan. Add the breadcrumb mixture and the garlic and pine kernels, season to taste with salt and pepper and cook over a low heat, stirring constantly, for 5 minutes, or until the breadcrumbs become golden, but not crisp. Remove the frying pan from the heat and cover to keep warm.

Bring a large heavy-based saucepan of lightly salted water to the boil. Add the pasta, return to the boil and cook for 8–10 minutes, or until tender but still firm to the bite.

Drain the pasta and transfer to a warmed serving dish. Drizzle with a little oil and toss to mix. Add the garlic breadcrumbs and toss again. Serve immediately with the grated pecorino cheese.

SERVES 4

350 g/12 oz fresh white breadcrumbs

4 tbsp finely chopped fresh flat-leaf parsley

1 tbsp snipped fresh chives

2 tbsp finely chopped fresh marjoram

3 tbsp olive oil, plus extra to serve

3–4 garlic cloves, finely chopped

55 g/2 oz pine kernels

450 g/1 lb dried tagliatelle, preferably a mixture of green and white

salt and pepper

55 g/2 oz freshly grated pecorino cheese, to serve

NEAPOLITAN CONCHIGLIE

Place the tomatoes in a large heavy-based saucepan. Add the wine, onion, carrot, celery, parsley and sugar and gradually bring to the boil, stirring frequently. Reduce the heat, partially cover and simmer, stirring occasionally, for 45 minutes, or until thickened.

Meanwhile, bring a large heavy-based saucepan of lightly salted water to the boil. Add the pasta, return to the boil and cook for 8–10 minutes, or until tender but still firm to the bite.

Rub the tomato sauce through a sieve with the back of a wooden spoon into a clean saucepan and stir in the marjoram. Reheat gently, stirring occasionally, for 1–2 minutes. Drain the pasta and transfer to a warmed serving dish. Pour the tomato sauce over the pasta and toss well. Sprinkle with Parmesan cheese and serve immediately.

SERVES 4

900 g/2 lb plum tomatoes, roughly chopped

150 ml/5 fl oz dry white wine

1 onion, chopped

1 carrot, chopped

1 celery stick, chopped

2 fresh flat-leaf parsley sprigs

pinch of sugar

350 g/12 oz dried conchiglie

1 tbsp chopped fresh marjoram

salt

freshly grated Parmesan cheese, to serve

FUSILLI WITH SUN-DRIED TOMATOES

Put the sun-dried tomatoes in a bowl, pour over the boiling water and leave to stand for 5 minutes. Using a slotted spoon, remove one third of the tomatoes from the bowl. Cut into bite-sized pieces. Put the remaining tomatoes and water into a blender and purée.

Heat the oil in a large frying pan over a medium heat. Add the onion and cook gently for 5 minutes, or until soft. Add the garlic and cook until just beginning to colour. Add the puréed tomato and the reserved tomato pieces to the pan. Bring to the boil, then simmer over a medium–low heat for 10 minutes. Stir in the herbs and season to taste with salt and pepper. Simmer for 1 minute, then remove from the heat.

Bring a large saucepan of lightly salted water to the boil. Add the pasta, bring back to the boil and cook for 8–10 minutes, or until tender but still firm to the bite. Drain and transfer to a warmed serving dish. Briefly reheat the sauce. Pour over the pasta, add the basil and toss well to mix. Sprinkle with the Parmesan cheese and serve immediately.

SERVES 4

85 g/3 oz sun-dried tomatoes (not in oil)

700 ml/1¼ pints boiling water

2 tbsp olive oil

1 onion, finely chopped

2 large garlic cloves, finely sliced

2 tbsp chopped fresh flat-leaf parsley

2 tsp chopped fresh oregano

1 tsp chopped fresh rosemary

350 g/12 oz dried fusilli

10 fresh basil leaves, shredded

salt and pepper

freshly grated Parmesan cheese, to serve

FETTUCCINE WITH OLIVES & PEPPERS

Heat the oil in a large heavy-based saucepan. Add the onion and cook over a low heat, stirring occasionally, for 5 minutes, or until softened. Add the olives, tomatoes and peppers and season to taste with salt and pepper. Cover and simmer gently over a very low heat, stirring occasionally, for 35 minutes.

Meanwhile, bring a large heavy-based saucepan of lightly salted water to the boil. Add the pasta, return to the boil and cook for 8–10 minutes, or until tender but still firm to the bite. Drain the pasta and transfer to a warmed serving dish.

Spoon the sauce onto the pasta and toss well. Serve immediately with the grated pecorino cheese.

SERVES 4

100 ml/3½ fl oz olive oil

1 onion, finely chopped

200 g/7 oz black olives, stoned and roughly chopped

400 g/14 oz canned chopped tomatoes, drained

2 red, yellow or orange peppers, deseeded and cut into thin strips

350 g/12 oz dried fettuccine

salt and pepper

freshly grated pecorino cheese, to serve

PAPPARDELLE WITH PUMPKIN SAUCE

Melt the butter in a large heavy-based saucepan. Add the shallots, sprinkle with a little salt, cover and cook over a very low heat, stirring occasionally, for 30 minutes.

Add the pumpkin pieces and season to taste with nutmeg. Cover and cook over a very low heat, stirring occasionally, for 40 minutes, or until the pumpkin is pulpy. Stir in the cream, Parmesan cheese and parsley and remove the saucepan from the heat.

Meanwhile, bring a large heavy-based saucepan of lightly salted water to the boil. Add the pasta, return to the boil and cook for 8–10 minutes, or until tender but still firm to the bite. Drain, reserving 2–3 tablespoons of the cooking water.

Add the pasta to the pumpkin mixture and stir in the reserved cooking water if the mixture seems too thick. Cook, stirring, for 1 minute, then transfer to a warmed serving dish and serve immediately with extra grated Parmesan cheese.

SERVES 4

55 g/2 oz butter

6 shallots, very finely chopped

800 g/1 lb 12 oz pumpkin, peeled, deseeded and cut into pieces

pinch of freshly grated nutmeg

200 ml/7 fl oz single cream

4 tbsp freshly grated Parmesan cheese, plus extra to serve

2 tbsp chopped fresh flat-leaf parsley

350 g/12 oz dried pappardelle

salt

PENNE WITH MIXED BEANS

Heat the oil in a large heavy-based frying pan. Add the onion, garlic, carrot and celery and cook over a low heat, stirring occasionally, for 5 minutes, or until the onion has softened.

Add the mixed beans, passata and chopped chervil to the frying pan and season the mixture to taste with salt and pepper. Cover and simmer gently for 15 minutes.

Meanwhile, bring a large heavy-based saucepan of lightly salted water to the boil. Add the pasta, return to the boil and cook for 8–10 minutes, or until tender but still firm to the bite. Drain the pasta and transfer to a warmed serving dish. Add the mixed bean sauce, toss well and serve immediately, garnished with extra chervil.

SERVES 4

1 tbsp olive oil

1 onion, chopped

1 garlic clove, finely chopped

1 carrot, finely chopped

1 celery stick, finely chopped

425 g/15 oz canned mixed beans, drained and rinsed

225 ml/8 fl oz passata

1 tbsp chopped fresh chervil, plus extra leaves to garnish

350 g/12 oz dried penne

salt and pepper

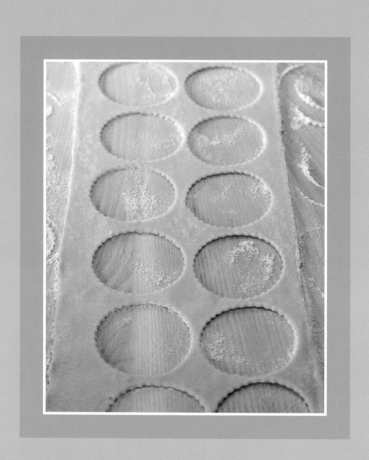

VEGETABLE CANNELLONI

Preheat the oven to 190°C/375°F/Gas Mark 5. Bring a large heavy-bottom saucepan of lightly salted water to the boil. Add the cannelloni tubes, return to the boil and cook for 8–10 minutes, or until tender but still firm to the bite. Transfer the pasta to a plate and pat dry with kitchen paper. Brush a large ovenproof dish with oil.

Cut the aubergine into small dice. Heat the oil in a frying pan over a medium heat. Add the aubergine and cook, stirring frequently, for about 2–3 minutes.

Add the spinach, garlic, cumin and mushrooms and reduce the heat. Season to taste with salt and pepper and cook, stirring, for about 2–3 minutes. Spoon the mixture into the cannelloni tubes and put into the dish in a single layer.

To make the sauce, heat the oil in a pan over a medium heat. Add the onion and garlic and cook for 1 minute. Add the tomatoes, sugar and basil and bring to the boil. Reduce the heat and simmer for about 5 minutes. Spoon the sauce over the cannelloni tubes.

Arrange the mozzarella cheese on top of the sauce and bake in the preheated oven for about 30 minutes, or until the cheese is golden brown and bubbling. Serve garnished with lamb's lettuce.

SERVES 4

12 dried cannelloni tubes

1 aubergine

125 ml/4 fl oz olive oil, plus extra for brushing

225 g/8 oz spinach

2 garlic cloves, crushed

1 tsp ground cumin

85 g/3 oz mushrooms, chopped

55 g/2 oz mozzarella cheese, sliced

salt and pepper

lamb's lettuce, to garnish

tomato sauce

1 tbsp olive oil

1 onion, chopped

2 garlic cloves, crushed

800 g/1 lb 12 oz canned chopped tomatoes

1 tsp caster sugar

2 tbsp chopped fresh basil

HOT TOMATO & CONCHIGLIE GRATIN

Put the onion, tomatoes and milk in a large heavy-based saucepan and bring just to the boil. Add the chillies, garlic, coriander and pasta, season to taste with salt and pepper and cook over a medium heat, stirring frequently, for 2–3 minutes.

Add just enough water to cover and cook, stirring frequently, for 8–10 minutes, until the pasta is tender but still firm to the bite. Meanwhile, preheat the grill.

Spoon the pasta mixture into individual flameproof dishes and sprinkle evenly with the cheese. Place under the grill for 3–4 minutes, until the cheese has melted. Serve immediately.

SERVES 4

1 onion, chopped

400 g/14 oz canned chopped tomatoes

225 ml/8 fl oz milk

1–2 red chillies, deseeded and finely chopped

1 garlic clove, finely chopped

pinch of ground coriander

280 g/10 oz dried conchiglie

85 g/3 oz Gruyère cheese, grated

salt and pepper

BEEF & MACARONI SOUFFLÉ

Preheat the oven to 190°C/375°F/Gas Mark 5. Heat the oil in a large heavy-based frying pan. Add the onion and cook over a low heat, stirring occasionally, for 5 minutes, or until softened. Add the beef and cook, breaking up the meat with a wooden spoon, until browned. Stir in the garlic, tomatoes and their can juices and tomato purée, then season to taste with salt and pepper. Bring to the boil, reduce the heat and simmer for 20 minutes, then remove the frying pan from the heat and leave to cool slightly.

Meanwhile, bring a large heavy-based saucepan of lightly salted water to the boil. Add the pasta, return to the boil and cook for 8–10 minutes, or until tender but still firm to the bite. Drain and reserve.

Lightly grease a 1.5-litre/2¾-pint soufflé dish with butter. Beat the egg yolks and add them to the meat sauce, then stir in the pasta. Whisk the egg whites until stiff peaks form, then fold into the sauce. Spoon the mixture into the dish, sprinkle with the grated Parmesan cheese and bake in the preheated oven for 45 minutes, or until well risen and golden brown. Sprinkle with extra grated Parmesan cheese and serve immediately.

SERVES 4

2 tbsp olive oil

1 large onion, chopped

225 g/8 oz fresh beef mince

1 garlic clove, finely chopped

400 g/14 oz canned chopped tomatoes

1 tbsp tomato purée

175 g/6 oz dried macaroni

butter, for greasing

3 eggs, separated

40 g/1½ oz freshly grated Parmesan cheese, plus extra to serve

salt and pepper

BEEF RAVIOLI

Heat the oil and half the butter in a large saucepan. Add the beef and cook over a medium heat for 8–10 minutes. Remove the beef from the pan. Reduce the heat and add the onion, celery and carrot to the pan. Cook for 5 minutes, until softened. Return the beef to the pan, add the wine and cook until reduced by two thirds. Combine the stock and tomato purée, stir into the pan and season. Cover and simmer very gently for 3 hours, until the meat is tender and the sauce has thickened. Remove the beef from the pan and leave to cool slightly.

Mix the breadcrumbs and half the Parmesan and stir in about half the sauce (discard the remaining sauce). Finely chop the beef and stir it into the breadcrumb mixture. Season and stir in the nutmeg, cinnamon and eggs.

Roll out the pasta dough on a lightly floured surface to 2–3 mm/ $\frac{1}{16}$–$\frac{1}{8}$ inch thick. Using a fluted 5-cm/2-inch biscuit cutter, stamp out rounds. Place about 1 teaspoon of the beef mixture in the centre of each round, brush the edges with water, and fold in half, pressing the edges to seal. Place on a floured tea towel and leave to stand for 30 minutes.

Bring a pan of salted water to the boil. Add the ravioli and cook for 5–8 minutes, until tender. Meanwhile, melt the remaining butter. Drain the ravioli and place in a serving dish. Pour over the melted butter, sprinkle with the remaining Parmesan and serve.

SERVES 6

3 tbsp olive oil

70 g/2½ oz butter

350 g/12 oz stewing beef, in a single piece

1 red onion, finely chopped

1 celery stick, finely chopped

1 carrot, finely chopped

150 ml/5 fl oz red wine

225 ml/8 fl oz beef stock

1 tbsp tomato purée

55 g/2 oz fresh breadcrumbs

4 tbsp freshly grated Parmesan cheese

pinch of freshly grated nutmeg

pinch of ground cinnamon

2 eggs, lightly beaten

1½ quantities Basic Pasta Dough (see page 8)

plain flour, for dusting

salt and pepper

CRAB RAVIOLI

Thinly slice the spring onions, keeping the white and green parts separate. Mix the green spring onions, crabmeat, ginger and chilli sauce to taste together in a bowl. Cover and chill.

Place the tomatoes in a food processor and process to a purée. Place the garlic, white spring onions and vinegar in a saucepan and add the puréed tomatoes. Bring to the boil, then reduce the heat and simmer for 10 minutes. Remove from the heat and reserve.

Divide the pasta dough in half and wrap 1 piece in clingfilm. Roll out the other piece on a lightly floured surface to a rectangle 2–3 mm/$\frac{1}{16}$–$\frac{1}{8}$ inch thick. Cover with a damp tea towel and roll out the other piece of dough to the same size. Place small mounds, about 1 teaspoon each, of the filling in rows 4 cm/1½ inches apart on a sheet of pasta dough. Brush the spaces between the mounds with beaten egg. Lift the second sheet of dough on top of the first and press down firmly between the pockets of filling, pushing out any air bubbles. Using a pasta wheel or sharp knife, cut into squares. Place on a floured tea towel and leave to stand for 1 hour.

Bring a large saucepan of lightly salted water to the boil. Add the ravioli and cook for 5 minutes. Remove with a slotted spoon and drain on kitchen paper. Gently heat the tomato sauce and whisk in the cream. Place the ravioli on serving plates, pour over the sauce, garnish with shredded spring onion and serve.

SERVES 4

6 spring onions

350 g/12 oz crabmeat

2 tsp finely chopped fresh ginger

$\frac{1}{8}$–$\frac{1}{4}$ tsp chilli sauce or Tabasco sauce

700 g/1 lb 9 oz tomatoes, peeled, deseeded and roughly chopped

1 garlic clove, finely chopped

1 tbsp white wine vinegar

1 quantity Basic Pasta Dough (see page 8)

plain flour, for dusting

1 egg, lightly beaten

2 tbsp double cream

salt

shredded spring onion, to garnish

INDEX